His Friend

PABLO DE SARASATE

Dedicatee

FANTASIE

(Introduction – Adagio – Scherzo – Andante – Finale)

for

the Violin
with Orchestra and Harp

with free Use of Scottish Folk Melodies

composed
by

MAX BRUCH.

—— Op. 46. ——

SCORE.

Publishers and Ownership for all Countries
N. SIMROCK, G.m.b.H. in BERLIN

1880

Scottish Fantasy

Fantasie für die Violine mit Orchester und Harfe
unter freier benutzung schottischer volksmelodien

Fantasy for violin with orchestra and harp
making free use of Scottish folk melodies

Einleitung (Introduction) - Adagio - Scherzo
Andante - Finale

Composed: *Berlin, 1879–1880*

Publisher: *N. Simrock, G.m.b.H., Berlin, 1880*

Première: *Sagebiel'schen Etablissement, Hamburg, 2ⁿᵈ October, 1880*
Conductor: Adolph Mehrkens
Soloist: Pablo de Sarasate

UK Première: Philharmonic Hall, Liverpool, 22ⁿᵈ February, 1881
Conductor: Max Bruch
Soloist: Joseph Joachim

Instrumentation: 2 Flauti (Flutes), 2 Oboi (Oboes), 2 Clarinetti (B)
(Clarinets in B♭) 2 Fagotti (Bassoons), 4 Corni (F) (Horns in F), 2
Trombe (D, Es) (Trumpets in D, E♭), 3 Tromboni (Trombones), Tuba
(Tuba), Timpani (Timpani), Gran Tamburo e Piatti (Bass Drum &
Cymbals), Violino principale (Solo Violin), Violino (Violin I, II), Viola
(Violas), Violoncello (Cellos), Basso (Basses), Arpa (Harp)

Approximate Duration (Complete Version): 32 minutes

A Few Notes

On

SCOTTISH FANTASY

by

ANDREW PHILLIPS

Trafalgar Press

Published by Trafalgar Press

British Library Cataloguing in Publication Data.
A catalogue record for this book is available from the British Library.

ISBN 978 1 3999 0011 9

'Melody is the soul of music'

Max Bruch

(1838–1920)

Original Title Page

AULD SCOTIA'S SANGS

By John Imlah
(1799-1846)

AULD SCOTIA'S SANGS! Auld Scotia's Sangs! — the strains o'
youth and yore! —
O lilt to me, and I will list — will list them o'er and o'er;
Though mak' me wae, or mak' me wud, — or changefu' as a child,
Yet lilt to me, and I will list — the 'native wood notes wild!'

They mak' me present wi' the past — they bring up, fresh and fair,
The Bonnie Broom o' Cowden Knowes, the Bush abune Traquair,
The Dowie Dens o' Yarrow, or the Birks o' Invermay,
Or Catrine's green and yellow Woods in autumn's dwining day!

They bring me back the holms and howes whar siller burnies shine,
The Lea-rig whar the gowans glint we pu'd in Auld Lang Syne;
And, mair than a', the Trystin' Thorn that blossom'd down the vale,
Whar gloamin' breathed sae sweetly — but far sweeter luve's fond
tale!

Now melt we o'er the lay that wails for Flodden's day o' dule, —
And now some rant will gar us loup like daffin' youth at Yule; —
Now o'er young luve's impassion'd strain our conscious heart will
yearn, —
And now our blude fires at the call o' Bruce o' Bannockburn!

O! lovely in the licht o' sang the Ettrick and the Tweed,
Whar shepherd swains were wont to blaw auld Scotia's
lyric reed; —
The Logan and the Lugar, too, but, hallow'd meikle mair,
The Banks and Braes o' bonnie Doun, — the Afton and the Ayr!

The hind whase hands are on the pleugh — the shepherd wi' his
crook —
The maiden o'er the milkin' pail, or by the ingle neuk,
Lo'e weel to croon auld Scotia's sangs — O may they ever sae!
And it may be a daffin' lilt — may be a dowie lay!

Though warldly grief and warldling's guile maun I like ithers dree,
Maun thole the sair saigh rive my breist — the het tear scald my e'e!
But let me list the melodies o' some o' Scotia's sangs,
And I will a' forget my waes — will a' forgie my wrangs!

O! born o' feeling's warmest depths — o' fancy's wildest dreams,
They're twined wi' monie lovely thochts, wi' monie lo'esome
themes;
They gar the glass o' memorie glint back wi' brichter shine
On far aff scenes, and far aff friends — and Auld Lang Syne!

Auld Scotia's Sangs! — Auld Scotia's Sangs! — her 'native wood
notes wild!'
Her monie artless melodies, that move me like a child;
Sing on — sing on! and I will list — will list them o'er and o'er, —
Auld Scotia's Sangs! — Auld Scotia's Sangs! — the sangs o' youth and
yore!

CONTENTS

LIST OF ILLUSTRATIONS

Front Cover photograph: Loch Coruisk, Isle of Skye, Scotland

Author's Note

All translations of articles from the Spanish and German are by the author.

A. P.

PREFACE

The reader who turns the pages of this small volume with the idea of finding in it a technical analysis of the *Scottish Fantasy* and a definitive account of its creation will, I fear, be disappointed. My intention has been a far more modest one.

This potpourri celebrates one of Max Bruch's most endearing works. His lyric musical interpretation of Scottish folksong has captured the imagination of violinists and music lovers for over 140 years.

It is hoped that these 'Notes' will be of interest to those with an abiding affection for the *Scottish Fantasy*, and that they might arouse the curiosity of those unfamiliar with the work.

Andrew Phillips
July 2021

Max Bruch

Figure of Max Bruch at Cologne City Hall

MAX BRUCH

'One of the most finished technicians of his generation'

H. C. Colles
(1879–1943)

M ax Bruch's misfortune as a composer was that he was working under the shadow of Beethoven and Brahms, the two colossi of 19th century German classical music. His work inclined towards the Romantic Classicism of Schumann and Mendelssohn and he was criticised by some for his conservatism and for failing to leave behind a style of composing that was rapidly changing.

Despite the more modern musical times in which he lived, the fact that he was successful in establishing himself as a composer of great merit says much about the originality, beauty and craftsmanship of his art. He was adept at almost every musical genre. German critics of his day predicted that posterity would remember him primarily for such cantatas and oratorios as *Frithjof: Szenen aus der Frithjof-Sage, Das Lied von der Glocke, Arminius* and *Das Feuerkreuz*, all of which were once in the repertoire of choral societies throughout Europe and America.

Max Bruch's genius was in his expressive powers, his mastery of harmony, counterpoint and instrumentation and his structural control. This was combined with impeccable taste. He composed some of the greatest choral works of the nineteenth century, three operas, many splendid orchestral works and numerous smaller pieces for various combinations of instruments.

Although he could acquit himself well on the 88 keys, Bruch was not drawn to the piano as a mode of musical expression. (This did not stop him from writing some pieces for the instrument, including his early *Fantasia* for two pianos and, in his final years, the Concerto for Two Pianos.) He much preferred the singing quality of the violin and the cello to 'that unmelodious keyed thing', and this predilection is reflected in his instrumental compositions. He saw the violin as supremely suited to the expression of fine, vocally conceived melody.

Max Christian Friedrich Bruch was born in Cologne in 1838, the son of August, a lawyer who later occupied the post of Police Chief. He inherited his musical ability and love of the *cantabile* style through his mother, a singing teacher with a good soprano voice, whom he described as 'musical through and through'. She gave him and his sister, Mathilde, their first lessons on the piano and she was to sow the seeds of her son's musical career.

As a young boy Bruch showed promising skill at painting. But music soon became his first love and, at the age of 9, he wrote his first musical composition for his mother's birthday. He received his first formal musical training under composer and pianist Ferdinand Hiller, to whom Robert Schumann devoted his piano concerto. Hiller thought highly of the young boy, and his prodigious talent brought him comparisons with the young Mozart and Mendelssohn. At the age of 14, as well as writing a symphony, he also won a scholarship that enabled him to study composition and piano in Cologne.

In 1858 Bruch embarked on his travels as a means to further his studies, broaden his education and, most importantly, to compose. He spent time in Leipzig, Berlin, Dresden, Vienna and Munich. Having failed to obtain a musical post in his own city, Cologne, he secured his first professional appointment in 1865 at the Royal Institute for Music in Coblenz. During this time, he worked on the Violin Concerto No. 1 in G minor Op. 26, the work that would ensure his fame and reputation as a composer but would eclipse much of his other work.

Bruch spent many productive years in the 1870s as a freelance composer in Berlin and Bonn. His career as a conductor progressed through appointments with various choral and orchestral societies at Sondershausen (1867), Berlin (1878), Liverpool (1880–83), and Breslau (1883–90). In 1890 he accepted a lectureship in composition at the Berlin Hochschule für Musik, working there until his retirement in 1910 and maintaining his position as a professor until his death.

Among Bruch's pupils in Berlin were Ottorino Respighi, Oskar Straus and Ernst Mielck (a gifted Finnish musician who died shortly before his 22nd birthday). Ralph Vaughan Williams studied composition with Bruch for a short time in 1897/98 and went on to join the English Folk Music Society and to write his delightful *English Folk Song Suite* (1923) and the *Fantasia on Greensleeves* (1934). So it may not be fanciful to suppose that some of Bruch's love of folk music may have rubbed off on his young student.

Bruch met Clara Tuczek, sixteen years his junior, during a concert tour in the summer of 1880 and, despite their age difference, they married in Berlin in January 1881. Bruch returned to Liverpool with his wife to resume his post with the Philharmonic Society. Clara Tuczek was born in 1854 in Berlin to an Austrian musical family. She used to sing occasionally at her husband's concerts. She died in Berlin on 27 August 1919, a year before her husband. They had three sons and a daughter, one son becoming a musician and another a noted artist.

Max Bruch died on 2 October 1920, at the age of 82, composing and thinking about music almost up to the end. In an obituary in the *Berliner Volks-Zeitung*, Dr L. Birnbaum wrote:

In his home in Friedenau, which he lived in for more than 30 years, the accomplished composer and former head of the championship class at the Hochschule für Musik, Max Bruch, honorary senator of the Academy of Arts, died. Bruch was known for his oratorios, of which *Achilleus*, *Odysseus* and *Frithjof* belonged to the permanent collection of all the major singing associations in Germany and abroad. The main works of his life, *Moses* and *Gustav Adolf*, made a strong, lasting impression when they were first performed by the Berlin Philharmonic Choir at the Singakademie. His wife Clara, née Tuczek, who recently preceded him in death, was a popular singer in her youth and interpreter of her husband's songs, some of which, like 'Lovely child. Can you tell me?' and the serenade from *Marino Falieri* 'You're not always 16 years old!' belonged to the music literature. Bruch, who, before moving to Berlin, was active as a choir and orchestra conductor in various cities in Germany, kept his art strictly on the basis of his classical models, of which he paid special tribute to Mendelssohn. In his younger years the deceased was active as a conductor of the Philharmonic Society in Liverpool. Since then he has enjoyed a special reputation in England; in 1893 the University of Cambridge awarded him an honorary Doctorate.

The deceased, who reached the venerable age of 82 and only recently had to experience the bitter pain of losing a flourishing son, the talented young painter Hans Bruch, far outlived the comrades of his time. His merits will also have to be recognized and honored by those who, in artistic terms, may have long since surpassed him.

Although he may not have been completely in tune with the musical zeitgeist of the era in which he worked, Max Bruch was confident in his own stature as a composer and was highly respected in the musical world as a master of his craft.

A large part of his output of over 100 published works has been forgotten and barely a handful of his instrumental compositions remain in the repertory. The public's love affair with his G minor Violin Concerto has not extended to a wider knowledge or appreciation of his work. Musical fashion and tastes change, but with the music of Bruch there is much to discover and to enjoy.

PABLO DE SARASATE

'Of course he is a musician to the tips of his fingers; but he is before all the man of his instrument'

Scots Observer, 1889

There emerged in Spain in the nineteenth century a prodigious talent that was to leave an indelible mark on the world of music. A country that had no great tradition in the art of violin playing (unlike, for example, France, Belgium and Germany) was to produce one of the leading virtuosos of his time, who captured the imagination of fellow musicians and the music-loving public alike. In his book *Master Violinists in Performance*, Henry Roth writes of Sarasate's artistry: 'Sarasate brought the bravura traditions of Paganini to a new level of refinement, tinctured with the flavor of his native Spain.'

Martín Melitón Sarasate y Navascués was born in Pamplona, Spain, in 1844. His father, Miguel, a military musician, was soon to recognise his son's extraordinary gift for music and the violin. Attesting to the child's precocity, he was later to recount that Martín knew the musical signs before the letters of the alphabet. At the age of seven he made his concert debut in La Coruña, where the young prodigy delighted both audience and critics.

In 1854, under the auspices of the Countess of Espoz y Mina, he travelled with his mother to Madrid to begin formal study. It was here that he was invited to play at the Royal Palace, after which an impressed Martín related in a letter to his father:

You can't imagine out how kind the Royal Family were to me. They wanted me to sit next to them. There was also the Princess and a number of gentlemen. Anyway, they were as nice as if they were my parents.

This informal audition would turn out to be an important event in his musical life; Queen Isabella II of Spain was to become one of his main supporters and patrons, granting him a scholarship to continue his training in Paris. In 1856 Sarasate left Madrid and entered the Paris Conservatoire, where he was a star pupil. His concert career started when he was fifteen and over the next decade he toured successfully throughout Europe. He was also becoming known for his own compositions, which were enthusiastically received. It was in the 1870s, when Sarasate was becoming established internationally, that he adopted 'Pablo' as his artistic name. In 1880 he made his first triumphal tour of Spain and Portugal. Over the next three decades he pursued a hectic programme of world-wide tours and performed in the USA, South America, Great Britain and Russia to universal acclaim. He continued his concertising in Europe from his homes in Paris and Biarritz. While still a student, Sarasate had asked Camille Saint-Saëns to write a work for him, and the result was the Violin Concerto No. 2 in C major, the first of numerous works composed specially for him. Sarasate had the honour of playing works written for him by Edouard Lalo (Violin Concerto in F major and Symphonie Espagnole), Polish violinist and composer Henryk Wieniawski (Violin Concerto No. 2 in D minor), Antonin Dvořák (*Mazurek for violin and orchestra)* and Scottish composer and conductor Alexander Mackenzie (Violin Concerto in C sharp minor, the suite for violin and orchestra, *Pibroch*[1], and the *Highland Ballad* for violin and orchestra.)

Max Bruch had been enchanted by Sarasate's interpretation of his G minor concerto and asked to meet Sarasate when he was in Germany. They became friends, and when asked by Sarasate for a concerto Bruch obliged by presenting him with his Violin Concerto No. 2 in

---

[1] Scottish bagpipe music involving variations on a martial theme or traditional dirge.

D minor Op. 44. Bruch wrote that it was 'a product of the inspiration aroused in me by his [Sarasate's] indescribably perfect performance of the first concerto'. Two years later, in 1879, Sarasate became the dedicatee of Bruch's *Scottish Fantasy*. As well as a celebrated interpreter, he was also a talented composer for the violin and wrote many successful pieces, most famously his *Zigeunerweisen* (Bohemian Aires), *Spanish Dances* and *Carmen Fantasy*.

As a musician Pablo de Sarasate was a unique national figure. He was much admired by his contemporaries, who spoke of him in glowing terms. Those fortunate enough to hear him play held him in the highest regard. There were many facets to his extraordinary talents. Not only was he a violinist of the highest order; he was also a composer, interpreter, teacher, promoter of musical creation and inspiration to many important composers of his day. His open and generous character earned him the friendship of prominent personalities of the time. He frequented the palaces of kings and the halls of nobility and counted figures such as Leo Tolstoy and Hermann Hesse among his acquaintances. James McNeill Whistler painted his portrait and he appeared in Arthur Conan Doyle's short story 'The Red-Headed League'.

Sarasate died in 1908 in Biarritz at the age of 64. Such was his fame that his death was reported in newspapers all over the world. An article in *The Scotsman*, 'Death of Sarasate. A great violinist', notes that 'Sarasate was not only an artist, but a unique artist. He was a distinctive personality. Joachim was an intelligent interpreter of the ideas of others. Sarasate was always Sarasate.' The *Berliner Morgenpost* declared that his death was 'a great loss to the musical world'.

Pablo de Sarasate

According to the esteemed violinist Tivadar Nachéz:

He was a great friend of mine and one of the most perfect players I have ever known, as well as one of the greatest *grand seigneurs* among violinists. His rendering of romantic works was exquisite. I have never heard them played as beautifully.

The Spanish violinist and conductor Enrique Fernández Arbós wrote:

Never have I heard a sound so brilliant, an execution so beautiful and so complete. He is one of those artists that, listening to them, cannot be analysed, for they produce a great effect on the public, without it being possible to know the means they employ to do it.

In his memoirs, Ignacy Jan Paderewski, Polish pianist, composer, and statesman, recalls:

He was charming personally and a marvellous artist, with irreproachable technique and the most beautiful violin tone imaginable - more beautiful than Joachim's.

As the French virtuoso Jacques Thibaud remembered:

He literally sang on the violin, like a nightingale. His purity of intonation was remarkable, and his technical facility was the most extraordinary that I have ever seen. He was the first to play the violin concertos of Saint-Saëns, Lalo and Max Bruch. They were all written for him, and I doubt whether they would have been composed had not Sarasate been there to play them. Of course, in his own Spanish music he was unexcelled - a whole school of violin playing was born and died with him!

THE SCOTTISH CONNECTION

Caledonia

By James Hogg
(1770-1835)

Caledonia! thou land of the mountain and rock,
Of the ocean, the mist, and the wind —
Thou land of the torrent, the pine, and the oak,
Of the roebuck, the hart, and the hind;
Though bare are thy cliffs, and though barren thy glens,
Though bleak thy dun islands appear,
Yet kind are the hearts, and undaunted the clans,
That roam on these mountains so drear!

A foe from abroad, or a tyrant at home,
Could never thy ardour restrain;
The marshall'd array of imperial Rome
Essay'd thy proud spirit in vain!
Firm seat of religion, of valour, of truth,
Of genius unshackled and free,
The muses have left all the vales of the south,
My loved Caledonia, for thee!

Sweet land of the bay and wild-winding deeps
Where loveliness slumbers at even,
While far in the depth of the blue water sleeps
A calm little motionless heaven!
Thou land of the valley, the moor, and the hill,
Of the storm and the proud rolling wave —
Yes, thou art the land of fair liberty still,
And the land of my forefathers' grave!

The Scottish Enlightenment of the 18th and early 19th centuries produced a blossoming of ideas and intellectual endeavours in philosophy, science, the arts, medicine and engineering. The reputations and achievements of the eminent men of the time fostered in Europe a new respect for Scotland and its recognition as a small but important nation. In 1762 Voltaire wrote that 'today it is from Scotland that we get rules of taste in all the arts, from epic poetry to gardening.'

Among the many outstanding figures at the forefront of this movement in all its diverse fields were David Hume and Adam Smith, Robert Adam and Allan Ramsay, James Boswell and Robert Burns, James Watt and Joseph Black.

At around the same time, the Romantic movement in Europe saw a burgeoning interest in Scotland and its literature. Many works of Scottish poetry were being translated into German and influencing musicians such as Mendelssohn, Beethoven and Haydn. The novels and poems of Sir Walter Scott, with their descriptions of Scotland's history and people and his evocation of an ancient land at the very edge of Europe ('the land of the mountain and the flood'[2]), were the inspiration for many of the leading composers of the day.

Berlioz, Bizet, Donizetti, Rossini and Schubert all wrote music based

---

[2] This description is from 'The Lay of the Last Minstrel', a long narrative poem by Sir Walter Scott. *The Land of the Mountain and the Flood* is a concert overture composed in 1887 by the 19-year-old Hamish MacCunn, a lifelong champion of Scottish folk music.

(sometimes loosely) on impressions of writings by Sir Walter Scott. Hector Berlioz gave us the *Grande Ouverture de Waverley* (Waveley: Grand Overture) in 1827, and his *Intrata di Rob-Roy Macgregor* (Rob Roy Overture) in 1831.

Bizet's *La jolie fille de Perth* is after Scott's *The Fair Maid of Perth* and Donizetti's *Lucia di Lammermoor* is based on *The Bride of Lammermoor*. Rossini's contribution was his pastiche opera *Ivanhoé*, completed in 1826.

Schubert composed seven settings of lyrics from 'The Lady of the Lake', The seven songs are five solo songs (three 'Ellen's Songs', 'Norman's Song' and 'Lay of the Imprisoned Huntsman') and two choruses, one for women, 'Coronach', and the other for men, 'Boat Song'. These are not the only verses by Scott which Schubert set to music; his other settings of Walter Scott's poems are 'Lied der Anne Lyle', D 830 (from *Montrose*) and 'Gesang der Norna', D 831 (from *The Pirate*).

Max Bruch was not the first German to be captivated by Scottish folk music, particularly as expressed in the songs of Robert Burns. In this he was preceded by Ludwig van Beethoven and Carl Maria von Weber. Composers such as Franz Joseph Haydn, Johann Nepomuk Hummel and Leopold Koželuch all produced Scottish folksong arrangements. The Scottish composer Alexander Mackenzie was inspired to write his *Burns - Second Scotch Rhapsody*.

A further Scottish musical association is through the country dance known as écossaise (French for 'Scottish' and possibly of Scottish origin), popular in France and England in the early 19th century. Stylised écossaises, mostly for piano, were composed by Beethoven, Schubert, Weber and Chopin.

Even Brahms was not immune to the lure of Scottish folksong. He wove Burns' 'My Heart's in the Highlands' into one of his sonatas and, it is said, could not get the melody out of his head while he was composing.

Though Bruch's interest in folk music was not limited to Scotland, he was impressed enough to write a number of compositions associated with the country and would have expressed a desire to visit it. Unlike Mendelssohn (whose journey to Scotland in 1829 resulted in *The Hebrides* Overture and his Scottish Symphony), Bruch was destined never to set foot on Scottish soil. Towards the end of his time in Liverpool he was offered the directorship of a conservatoire that was to be established in Edinburgh, and also the directorship of concerts in Edinburgh and Glasgow. The salary was substantially more than he was receiving with the Liverpool Philharmonic Society. He was to be disappointed, however, when the Scottish authorities failed to raise the necessary funds and were forced to abandon the plan.

It is fitting that Pablo de Sarasate, to whom the *Scottish Fantasy* is dedicated, should have visited Scotland on more than one occasion, giving recitals in Edinburgh, Glasgow, Dundee and Aberdeen. According to accounts, he would include performances of music written for him by his friend Alexander Mackenzie, himself a violinist.

SCOTTISH ORCHESTRA CONCERTS.

ORCHESTRAL CONCERT,
ST. ANDREW'S HALL,
MONDAY, 27TH NOVEMBER, AT 8.

SOLO VIOLINIST—
SENOR SARASATE
(Only appearance in Glasgow this Season).

PROGRAMME.

OVERTURE, "Genoveva".............................*Schumann*
SYMPHONIE ESPAGNOLE for Violin and Orchestra .... *Lalo*
SYMPHONY No. 2, in D (Op. 73).........................*Brahms*
RONDO CAPRICCIOSO for Violin and Orchestra..*Saint-Saens*
HUNGARIAN RHAPSODY No. 2, in D ....*Liszt*

ORCHESTRA OF 76 PERFORMERS.
CONDUCTOR........................MR HENSCHEL.

Tickets—7s, 3s 6d, 2s, 1s—At PATERSON'S, 152 Buchanan St.

Glasgow Evening Post, 24 November 1893

Musical composition inspired by Scottish writings was not just a cultural phenomenon of the 19th century. Between the 1940s and 1970s the composer Benjamin Britten wrote settings of texts by the Scottish poets Robert Burns and William Soutar as well as arrangements of some of Burns' songs. These pieces were scored for tenor voice with piano and traditional harp accompaniment. In 1941 he composed his Scottish Ballad for two pianos and orchestra, based on Scottish tunes. As in Bruch's *Scottish Fantasy*, it incorporates a lamenting funeral march and a lively dance. The prolific English composer Malcolm Arnold wrote various arrangements of his Four Scottish Dances (1957), and many 20th century Scottish composers, such as Ian Hamilton, Erik Chisholm and Ronald Stevenson, were influenced by the traditional music and song of their native land.

Robert Burns
1759–1796

SONGS OF SCOTLAND AND THE INFLUENCE OF ROBERT BURNS

'How is he [Burns] great, except through the circumstance that the whole songs of his predecessors lived in the mouth of the people, that they were, so to speak, sung at his cradle; that as a boy he grew up amongst them, and the high excellence of these models so prevailed him that he had therein a living basis on which he could proceed further?'

Conversations of Goethe
Johann Peter Eckermann, 1836

A song is generally the earliest form in which the literary taste of a nation is to be found, and the collected songs of a country placed before a critical reader is probably the most severe test of its excellence in literature. To write a mere song, or words to accompany a given air is a comparatively easy matter, but to write one which will touch the heart or the passions, and stand the test of time, after all the best test of poetic merit, is a gift comparatively rare. To be popular with the masses, its language must be simple and unaffected: nothing, in Scottish Song especially, is more nonsensical than the introduction of Phillis, Adonis, Miranda, or Strephon, or any of these classical beauties and exquisites. To be remembered, it must be short; and its sentiments whether amorous, bacchanalian, warlike, or domestic, must not be extravagant, but rather given with subdued power, while to please the critical reader its rhyme must be smooth and its rhythm faultless. That these conditions are fulfilled by the majority of our best Scotch songs may be seen by glancing at the collection here submitted to the public. To select a few, what could be finer or more pleasing to Critics and readers than 'O waly waly up the bank', 'Auld Robin Gray', 'I've heard a lilting', 'Brume o' the Cowdenknowes', 'Tam Glen', 'My Nannie's awa', 'Land o' the Leal', 'Lucy's Flittin', and many others? There is one thing which cannot fail to strike the reader of these songs, and it is the fact that the great majority of our best songs are from the pens of writers born in the poorer ranks of society, and whose education was generally comparatively imperfect. Ramsay, Burns, Allan Cunningham, Mayne, Tanhahill, Hogg, Gall, Laidlaw, may serve to illustrate this in the later period of the annals of our song. For the earlier period the song writers are generally unknown, but from various circumstances we must infer that the same fact is visible here also, especially when we remember that in the works of Sir David Lindsay, Gawain Douglas, or Dunbar, we do not find any piece which could be included in a collection of Scottish song; and assuredly these writers give us no name distinguished in their time for excellence in this department of their craft. Why this should be, we leave some future investigator into the Curiosities of Literature to determine.

The Songs of Scotland, 1871

Bruch's extensive knowledge of and fondness for vocal composition would naturally draw him to a country's traditional songs. In Scottish folk music, Bruch found an extremely rich source of material with which to give free reign to his musical imagination. And it was largely through Robert Burns' endeavours that Bruch was able to find the means with which he could indulge his proclivity for melodic expression. Two of the earliest collections of Scots songs were Allan Ramsay's *Tea-Table Miscellany* of 1724 and the *Orpheus Caledonius* of 1725 by William Thomson, where many of the songs appeared in print for the first time. But Bruch's source was

James Johnson's *The Scots Musical Museum*, published in six volumes from 1787, in which Robert Burns functioned as a compiler and a major contributor.

Of the many dozens of Scottish folk songs available, Bruch uses themes from some of the most well-known and develops them in the *Scottish Fantasy*'s four movements. Three of these folk songs are by Burns, one is by the Scottish poet and playwright Allan Ramsay, while another is an earlier work of unknown origin.

Robert Burns was born in 1759, two years after the first printed collection of Scottish dance music, and six years before Thomas Percy's *Reliques of Ancient Poetry* was published. He died in 1796, his life bounded by the last half of the eighteenth century, which was the classical age of the revival of popular poetry. He was a close contemporary of Mozart and, in his own art, showed a similar degree of fecundity. Burns reputation lies not just in his verse but in his musical ability as an expert and an authority on Scottish Song.

Burns knew more of the popular music of his country than any man of his time, and he is unique among distinguished poets in writing for pre-existing music. He wrote original songs for specific melodies previously selected and studied, and he had to consider their musical as well as their literal interpretation. His skill was in finding suitable words and rhymes to fit some favourite melodies.

He was unique as a reviver of old songs, taking mere fragments of an air – or a word, a line, a chorus - and creating a finished song of music and verse. In short, Burns embodied the whole cycle of Scottish Song, both as a writer of original songs and as a reconstructor of the songs of the past.

Seven-eighths of his songs were written during the last nine years of his life, when he was an unsuccessful farmer and a gauger, riding often two hundred miles a week in the discharge of his duty. He often wrote in uncomfortable country inns, with the distraction of callers, and this was typical of the conditions in which he produced many of his best songs and letters. His lowly circumstances make the quantity and originality of his work all the more remarkable. It is true to say that, in his short life, Burns established the folk music of Scotland as well as its vernacular poetry – and he did so conscientiously and with dedication.

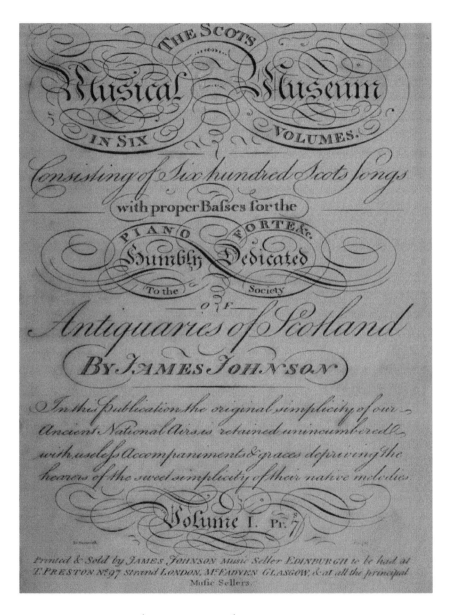

The Scots Musical Museum, 1787

SCOTTISH FANTASY

*'Many a banner spread flutters above your head,
Many a crest that is famous in story;
Mount and make ready, then, sons of the mountain glen —
Fight for your queen and the old Scottish glory.'*

Sir Walter Scott
(1771–1832)

There appears to be much confusion on the question of when and where the *Scottish Fantasy* was composed and premièred: various books, recording notes and websites give the place as Berlin, London, Hamburg and Liverpool, the date as 1880. 1881 and 1883, and the soloist as Sarasate and Joachim.

In a letter to the author dated 3 January 1986, Rex Bawden, music critic of the Liverpool Daily Post and Echo, writes:

> I have now checked both with the Philharmonic's own archives, and with the ultimate authority, the New Grove Dictionary. It is clear from the former that the British première took place in Liverpool on 22 February 1881, and was advertised as such, with Joachim as soloist.
> But Grove, while not specifying that Sarasate was the actual soloist, states that the world première was in Berlin in 1880, and that the work was dedicated to Sarasate.

It appears that the 'ultimate authority' is also incorrect. The *Scottish Fantasy* was composed in Berlin during the winter of 1879 and 1880.

It was premièred at the 1880 Musikfest in Hamburg, when the soloist was Pablo de Sarasate. The concert was part of a three-day festival celebrating 25 years since the foundation of the Hamburg Bach Society. The day after the concert, a review appeared in the newspaper *Hamburger Nachrichten*:

> Herr Pablo de Sarasate, who has appeared here many times and who is highly regarded for his extraordinary virtuosity and esteemed Spanish violin art, entered the platform to a loud and warm reception. The artist presented the completely new 'Schottische Fantasie' for violin and orchestra by Max Bruch, performed for the first time in a German concert hall. 'Fantasie' deserves its title only because of the partly lyrical, partly dance-like Scottish motifs chosen for the four movements. The artistic vision and the character of the whole work lacks a particularly national identity; what one hears is Bruch's well-known music, with its great virtues of artistic and poetic contemplation, colourful orchestration and phraseology. The solo part, which encourages modern violin technique and is in contrast to German violin playing, is in symphonic interaction with the richly thought-out orchestration, both factors combining into an effective harmonic whole. Herr Pablo de Sarasate, whose particular skills have certainly been an influence in the writing, is the masterly solo voice.
>
> He was generously thanked for his singular artistry by the listeners, but they were even more exuberant when, with piano accompaniment (Mr Otto Goldschmidt from Mainz), he played his dainty Spanish pieces, the *Romanza* and the *Zapateado*, with grace and elegance and with interspersed technical tricks and embellishments in the Romance violin style. To the joy of the enthusiastic audience he added to these amiable pieces a Nocturn by Chopin, arranged for violin, after which cheers broke out again with the same degree of intensity.

The first UK performance of the work took place in 1881, under the direction of Bruch himself, not long after he had taken up his appointment with the Liverpool Philharmonic Society. The soloist was the Hungarian virtuoso Joseph Joachim.

Although never considered a work of major importance by musicologists, the *Scottish Fantasy* is nevertheless one of Bruch's most beautiful and finely structured compositions. In it he finds a means of expression that is lyrical and poetic. Amid the tender melodies, the violin, harp and orchestra are given ample opportunity to display their capabilities in a varied and technically complex work.

Bruch was not completely happy at the reception to his new work. Though liked by the public, it was less favourably received by the critics. Bruch wrote that the *Scottish Fantasy* 'which even gives pleasure to people like Brahms and Joachim, is torn apart everywhere by the mob of critics'. In its item 'A Scotch Violin Concerto' following a concert in London in 1883, the *Edinburgh Evening News* was far from complimentary about the work:

An extraordinary composition, entitled a violin concerto on Scottish melodies, by Herr Max Bruch (says a London correspondent) was played by Señor Sarasate at the last Philharmonic concert. The novel point of the piece is that there are no subjects proper, the themes being popular Scottish melodies heavily disguised as only a foreigner could disguise them. The composer happily gave the analytical programme writer a clue to the identity of the melodies used, as otherwise they might not have been readily recognised. The chief theme of the first movement is 'Old Robin Morris'; in the second movement appears 'Lochaber no more'; in the third 'There was a Lad was born in Kyle'; and in the last, 'Scots wha hae' and 'Caller Herrin'.[3] Not even the ability of the violinist, Señor Sarasate, could save this distortion of Scottish tunes, and an attempt to recall the composer

---

[3] 'Lochaber no more', 'There was a Lad was born in Kyle' and 'Caller Herrin' all appear in collections of old Scottish songs, but it is unclear whether or to what extent Bruch used them in the *Scottish Fantasy*.

elicited signs of disapproval such as are rarely heard at a Philharmonic concert.

Like other German composers (including Mendelssohn, one of his musical idols) Max Bruch had a strong interest in Scottish folk lore, music and song. It is said that it was the novels and poetry of the celebrated Scottish writer Sir Walter Scott that provided the inspiration for the *Scottish Fantasy*. Bruch had earlier shown an interest in the writer's 'Lady of the Lake' and in 1874 had started a piece, *Das Feuerkreuz* ('The Fiery Cross'), based on the poem. As someone with a strong vocal heritage, Bruch would naturally be drawn to the folksong of Scotland and to find his muse, if unwittingly, in the poet Robert Burns, whose efforts were instrumental in the collection and preservation of these ancient tunes and ditties.

The *Scottish Fantasy* is not simply a medley of Scottish tunes; it is a skilfully crafted symphonic work embracing authentic and original material. More than just a composer's picture postcard of Scotland, it is also a musical echo of the Scottish Bards. Bruch decided to call the work a 'Fantasy' rather than a concerto, and in a letter to the publisher Simrock in 1880 wrote: 'The title 'Fantasy' is very general, and as a rule refers to a short piece rather than to one in several movements (all of which, moreover, are fully worked-out and developed). However, this work cannot properly be called a concerto because the form of the whole is so completely free, and because folk melodies are used.' During its writing, Bruch conferred with violinist Joseph Joachim (to whom he had dedicated the G Minor Concerto) on technical aspects of the solo part.

As far as the folk idiom is concerned, the *Scottish Fantasy* was not Bruch's last word on the subject. Ten years later he would write the autumnal *Adagio on Celtic Themes* for cello and orchestra Op. 56, this time using Scottish and Irish melodies; and two of his final orchestral opuses were the Suite on Russian Folk Melodies Op. 79b and the *Serenade for String Orchestra* (on Swedish Melodies) Op. posth. (1916).

Musikfest

zur Jubiläumsfeier der Bach-Gesellschaft in Hamburg am 30. September, 1. und 2. October d. J.,
Abends 7 Uhr, im Sagebiel'schen Etablissement.
Dirigent: Herr **Adolph Mehrkens.**

Mitwirkende: Frau **A. Esslpoff** aus **Wien** (Pianoforte), Herr **P. de Sarasate** aus
Madrid (Violine), Frau **M. Otto-Alvsloben** aus **Dresden**, Frl. **E. Scheel** von hier (Sopran),
Frl. **A. Asmann** aus **Berlin** (Alt); die Herren **W. Candidus** aus **Frankfurt** (Tenor),
E. Hungar aus **Dresden** (Baß), Frl. **J. Herrmann** aus **Lübeck** (Harfe), **H. Degenhardt**
und **C. Armbrust** von hier (Orgel) und Mitglieder der Bachgesellschaft. Concertmeister: Die
Herren **Japha** aus **Köln**, **Engel** aus **Oldenburg**, **Beer** und **Schloming** von hier.

☞ Chor und Orchester über **500** Personen. ☜

Programm:

1. Tag: (Unter Mitwirkung sämmtlicher Gesangsolisten, sowie der Herren Degenhardt und Armbrust.)
a) Bach. Toccata in d-moll, zur Einweihung der neuen, großen Concertorgel.
b) Händel. Salomo. Oratorium für Soli, Chor, Orgel u. Orchester, bearbeitet v. Ad. Mehrkens.

II. Tag:	**III. Tag:**
1) Bach. Magnificat für 5 Soli, Chor u. Orchester, bearbeitet von R. Franz.	1) Liszt. Einleitung und Chöre mit Soli aus dem Oratorium Christus.
2) Gluck. Ouverture zu Iphigenie in Aulis.	2) Mendelssohn. Ouverture zu den Hebriden.
3) Weber. Duett aus Euryanthe für Sopr. u. Tenor.	3) Schubert, Jensen. Lieder für Mezzo-Sopran.
4) Schumann. Concert in a-moll für Pft m. Orchester.	4) Bruch. Schottische Fantasie für Violine (neu).
5) Brahms. Die Heimath. Soloquartett mit Pft.	5) Hiller, Reinecke, Holstein. Duette.
6) Chopin, Rubinstein. Solostücke für Pft.	6) Sarasate u. s. w. Solostücke für Violine.
7) Wagner. Kaisermarsch, für Chor u. Orchester.	7) Beethoven. Sinfonie in a-dur, für Orchester.

Abonnements à 12 M. für alle 3 Tage, sowie Einzelkarten à 5 M. (beides nummerirter Platz)
sind nur in der Musikalienhandlung des Herrn Böhme zu haben.

Nichtnummerirte Karten à 3 M., sowie Karten à 2 M. zu den

3 Hauptproben

1) am Mittwoch, den 29. September, Abends 7 Uhr, 2) Donnerstag, den 30. September,
Morgens 11 Uhr, 3) Freitag, den 1. October, Morgens 11 Uhr, welche unter Mitwirkung sämmt-
licher Solisten im Sagebiel'schen Etablissement stattfinden, sind in den Musikalienhandlungen der Herren
Böhme, Cranz, Haring, Hoffmann, Jowien, Leopoldt, Schuberth, Hentze (St. Georg) und Mudrich
Nachf. (Altona) zu haben.

NB. Der Reinertrag ist für den Kirchenbau vor dem Dammthor und für die Musiker-
Pensions- und Wittwencassen bestimmt. **Das Comite.**

Scottish Fantasy at the Hamburg Musikfest, 1880

The *Scottish Fantasy* consists of an introduction and four movements, each with a contrasting mood.

Introduction: Grave

The work opens in sombre fashion with a funeral march (*Grave*).[4] This leads quickly into a quasi-recitative dialogue, with a series of emotional (*appassionato*) violin passages and orchestral responses.

I. Adagio cantabile

An orchestral tutti provides a gentle transition into the Adagio, punctuated by a plaintive horn call in the distance. The harp (representing the bardic instrument) plays a prominent part here, before the soloist enters to sing the main theme. This is a richly scored melody with violin in dialogue with the harp. The movement is brought to a quiet close as orchestra and soloist die away (*morendo*).

---

[4] A similar device is employed in the first movement of Bruch's Violin Concerto No. 2, also written for Sarasate.

It is usually stated that the theme of the Adagio cantabile is based on the ballad 'Auld Rob Morris'. Bruch had taken 'Der Alte Rob Morris' and arranged a four-part setting of it in his a *Zwölf Schottische Volkslieder (Twelve Scottish Folk Songs)* in 1863. At the opening of the Adagio the strain of 'Auld Rob Morris' is heard, while the main section uses the ancient air 'Through the Wood, Laddie'.

II. Scherzo
Allegro - (Dance) - Animato – Adagio - Allegro - Adagio

This movement, a lively dance in sonata-like form, incorporates the folk tune 'The Dusty Miller'.[5]

The repeated phrase from strings and horn at the start of the Allegro imitates the drone of the bagpipe.[6] Rhythmic sections, variations and modulations develop the theme, but with tunefulness to the fore. In a display of digital virtuosity, solo flute joins solo violin to play a fast passage in unison.

A closing cadence recalls a fragment of the Adagio.

---

[5] The book *Early Scottish Melodies* mentions that the song is contained in *Walsh's Compleat Country Dancing Master* and 'therefore the tune must be English'.

[6] It is thought that the bagpipe was introduced into Scotland not as a Roman importation but as the result of two Irish colonisations: the first, under Cairbre Riada, in 120 CE; and the second, under Fergus, Lome, and Angus, the sons of Erc, about the year 506 CE. In legend it became the distinctive sound of the Scots in battle.

This is followed by a sorrowful connecting passage led by both soloist and re-awakened harp and opening into the Andante sostenuto.

III. Andante sostenuto

Bruch uses the sweet, touching love song 'I'm a' doun for lack o' Johnnie' in this movement. The theme is shaped into a lovely reverie for solo violin, the *cantilena* gradually carrying the movement to a choppy middle section, where harp matches violin in virtuosity. A delicate, expressive passage ensues, heralding a short, eloquent tutti, before the soloist takes up the impassioned melody, becoming softly introspective as the movement draws to its close.

IV. Finale
Allegro guerriero - [coda] Adagio - Allegro

This rousing movement has the martial song 'Scots wha ha'e' as its warlike (*guerriero*) motif. Legend has it that this was sounded by Robert the Bruce at the Battle of Bannockburn in 1314.

The movement opens with a display of triple stopping by the soloist accompanied by the harp.

Two subjects dominate, with repeated dramatic and melodic variations and exchanges. A final recapitulation of the main theme and refrain signal the conclusion of the movement, introduced by an inspired coda, and permitting one last display of bravura fingerwork by the soloist.

There follows a brief, nostalgic echo back to the Adagio before the work is brought to a robust end.

THEMES USED IN SCOTTISH FANTASY

The genius of the Scots has in nothing shone more conspicuous than in Poetry and Music. Of the first, the Poems of Ossian composed in an age of rude antiquity, are sufficient proof. The peevish doubt entertained by some of their authenticity, appears to be the utmost refinement of scepticism.[7] As genuine remains of *Celtic* Poetry, the Poems of Ossian will continue to be admired as long as there shall remain a taste for the *sublime and beautiful*. The Scottish Music does no less honour to the genius of the country.

The old Scottish songs have always been admired for the wild pathetic sweetness which distinguishes them from the music of every other country. From their artless simplicity, it is evident, that the Scottish melodies are derived from very remote antiquity. The simplicity and wildness of several of our old Scottish melodies, denote them to be the production of a pastoral age and country, and prior to the use of any musical instrument beyond that of a very limited scale of a few natural notes, and prior to the knowledge of any rules of artificial music. This conjecture, if solid, must carry them up to a high period of antiquity. The most ancient of the Scottish songs, still preserved, are extremely simple, and void of all art. They consist of one measure only, and have no second part, as the later or more modern airs have. They must, therefore, have been composed for a very simple instrument, such

---

[7] The 3rd century Scottish bard Ossian is believed to be the invention of his 18th century 'translator' James Macpherson.

as the shepherd's reed or pipe, of few notes, and of the plain diatonic scale, without using the semitones, or sharps and flats. The distinguishing strain of our old melodies is plaintive and melancholy; and what makes them soothing and affecting, to a great degree, is the constant use of the concordant tones, the third and fifth of the scale, often ending upon the fifth, and some of them on the sixth of the scale. By this artless standard some of our old Scottish melodies may be traced.

A Selection of the most Favourite Scots Songs
W. Tytler

Through The Wood, Laddie
By Allan Ramsay
Air: *Through the Wood*

O Sandy, why leav'st thou thy Nelly to mourn?
Thy presence could ease me,
When naething could please me;
Now dowie I sigh on the bank o' the burn,
Or through the wood, laddie, until thou return.

Though woods now are bonnie, and mornings are clear,
While lav'rocks are singing,
And primroses springing;
Yet nane o' them pleases my eye or my ear,
When through the wood, laddie, ye dinna appear.

That I am forsaken, some spare not to tell;
I'm fash'd wi' their scornin',
Baith e'enin' an' mornin';
Their jeering gaes aft to my heart wi' a knell,
When through the wood, laddie, I wander mysel'.

Then stay, my dear Sandy, nae langer away;
But quick as an arrow,
Haste, haste to thy marrow,
Wha's living in languor till that happy day,
When through the wood, laddie, thegither we'll gae!

Through The Wood
Songs of the Affections
From Ramsay's *Tea-Table Miscellany*, 1724.

AULD ROB MORRIS

by Robert Burns
Air: *Jock the Laird's Brither*

There's auld Rob Morris that wons in yon glen,
He's the king o' guid fellows an' wale o' auld men.
He has gowd in his coffers, he has owsen an' kine,
An' ae bonnie lassie, his darling and mine.

She's fresh as the morning, the fairest in May;
She's sweet as the ev'ning amang the new hay;
As blythe and as artless as the lambs on the lea,
An' dear to my heart as the light to my e'e.

But, oh! She's an heiress, auld Robin's a laird,
An' my daddie has naught but a cot-house an' yard;
A wooer like me maunna hope to come speed,
The wounds I must hide that will soon be my dead.

The day comes to me, but delight brings me nane;
The night comes to me, but my rest it is gane:
I wander my lane like a night-troubled ghaist,
And I sigh as my heart it wad burst in my breast.

Oh, had she but been of a lower degree,
I then might ha'e hop'd she wad smil'd upon me!
Oh, how past describing had then been my bliss,
As now my distraction no words can express!

In these beautiful verses of his love song with the same title, Burns preserves the first two lines of an old satirical song (below) which appeared in the *Tea-Table Miscellany* of 1724. In a letter to George Thomson, Burns wrote: 'I have partly taken your idea of "Auld Rob Morris". I have adopted the two first verses, and am going on with the song on a new plan, which promises pretty well.'

AULD ROB MORRIS
Moral and Satirical Songs
From Ramsay's *Tea-Table Miscellany*, 1724.

MOTHER.
Auld Rob Morris, that wons in yon glen,
He's the king o' guid fellows, and wale o' auld men;
He has fourscore o' black sheep, and fourscore too,
Auld Rob Morris is the man ye maun lo'e.

DAUGHTER.
Hauld your tongue, mother, and let that abee,
For his eild and my eild can never agree;
They'll never agree, and that will be seen,
For he is fourscore, and I'm but fifteen.

MOTHER

Hauld your tongue, dochter, and lay by your pride,
For he is the bridegroom, and ye'se be the bride;
He shall lie by your side, and kiss you too;
Auld Rob Morris is the man ye maun lo'e.

DAUGHTER.

Auld Rob Morris, I ken him fu' weel,
His back it sticks out like ony peat creel;
H's out-shinn'd, in-knee'd, and ringle-eyed too;
Auld Rob Morris is the man I'll ne'er lo'e.

MOTHER.

Though auld Rob Morris be an elderly man,
Yet his auld brass will buy you a new pan;
Then, dochter, ye shouldna be sae ill to shoe,
For auld Rob Morris is the man ye maun lo'e.

DAUGHTER.

But auld Rob Morris I never shall ha'e,
His back is sae stiff, and his beard is grown grey;
I had rather die than live wi' him a year,
Sae mair o' Rob Morris I never will hear.

HEY, THE DUSTY MILLER
By Robert Burns
Tune: *The Dusty Miller*

This cheerful old air was, in former times, frequently played as a single hornpipe in the dancing schools of Scotland. The verses to which it is adapted in the *Musical Museum*, beginning 'Hey, the dusty miller, and his dusty coat,' are a fragment of the old ballad, with a few verbal alterations by Burns.

Hey, the dusty miller,
And his dusty coat;
He will win a shilling,
Or he spend a groat.
Dusty was the coat,
Dusty was the colour,
Dusty was the kiss
That I got frae the miller.

Hey, the dusty miller,
And his dusty sack;
Leeze me on the calling
Fills the dusty peck —
Fills the dusty peck,
Brings the dusty siller;
I wad gi'e my coatie
For the dusty miller.

The Dusty Miller

I'M A' DOUN FOR LACK O' JOHNNIE

A song long popular north of the Tay, the authorship of the words and air is unknown.

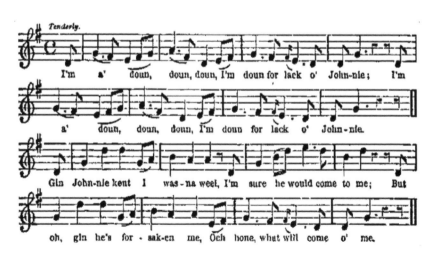

I'm a' doun, doun, doun,
  I'm doun for lack o' Johnnie;
I'm a' doun, doun, doun,
  I'm doun for lack o' Johnnie.

Gin Johnnie kent I wasna weel,
  I'm sure he would come to me;
But oh, gin he's forsaken me,
  Och hone, what will come o' me.

I'm a' doun, doun, doun,
  I'm doun for lack o' Johnnie;
I'm a' doun, doun, doun,
  I'm doun for lack o' Johnnie.

I sit upon an auld feal-sunk,
  I spin and greet for Johnnie;
But gin he's gi'en me the begunk,
  Och hone, what will come o' me.

The Battle of Bannockburn, 1314

BANNOCKBURN
ROBERT BRUCE'S ADDRESS TO HIS ARMY
(SCOTS WHA HA'E)

This heroic ode, written by Burns in 1793 to the tune of 'Hey, tuttie taitie', has been adopted by universal consent as the national patriotic song of Scotland. It was sent to George Thomson for insertion in his collection, but he chose to set the ode to the tune of 'Lewie Gordon' as being an air more worthy of such spirited words. He later changed his mind, however, and restored the air that Burns had originally intended.

On the origin of the songs, Burns wrote in a letter to Thomson:

There is a tradition which I have met with in many places of Scotland, that the air of 'Hey, tuttie taitie' was Robert Bruce's march at the battle of Bannockburn. This thought, in my yesternight's evening walk, warmed me to a pitch of enthusiasm on the theme of liberty and independence, which I threw into a kind of Scottish ode, that one might suppose to be the royal Scot's address to his heroic followers on that eventful morning.

The battle of Bannockburn, which took place in 1314, marked the culmination of the wars that had been waged between England and Scotland for many years. The English were routed, and the hero of the battle, Robert Bruce, became the first king of independent Scotland. Sporadic war with England continued until 1328, when the Treaty of Northampton recognised the independence of Scotland and Bruce's right to the throne.

Burns was 34 when he wrote the poem. The farm he leased in Dumfries had failed and he had obtained a position as an excise officer, while still contributing his verses and songs to editors. He died from heart failure just three years later, in 1896, and has ever since been revered as Scotland's national poet.

Scots Wha Ha'e
by Robert Burns
Tune: *Hey, tuttie taitie*

Scots, wha hae wi' Wal- lace bled, Scots,wham Bruce has af- ten led! Wel-

come to your go- ry bed, or to vic- to- ry! Now's the day an' now's the hour, See

the front of bat- tle lour, See ap- proach proud Ed- ward's pow'r, Chains and sla- ve- ry!

Scots, wha ha'e wi' Wallace bled,
Scots, wham Bruce has aften led;
Welcome to your gory bed,
Or to glorious victorie!

Now's the day and now's the hour;
See the front o' battle lower;
See approach proud Edward's power —
Edward! chains and slaverie!

Wha will be a traitor knave?
Wha can fill a coward's grave?
Wha sae base as be a slave?
Traitor! coward! turn and flee!

Wha for Scotland's king and law,
Freedom's sword will strongly draw,
Free-man stand, or free-man fa',
Caledonian! on wi' me!

By oppression's woes and pains!
By your sons in servile chains!
We will drain our dearest veins,
But they shall be — shall be free!

Lay the proud usurpers low!
Tyrants fall in every foe!
Liberty's in every blow!
Forward! let us do, or die!

Bruch House, Liverpool

Detail on Commemorative Plaque at Bruch House

MAX BRUCH IN LIVERPOOL

Max Bruch first appeared in Liverpool in 1877 as guest conductor for a performance of one of his own works, the secular oratorio *Odysseus*. He made a successful return in 1879 with his cantata *Das Lied von der Glocke* ('The Song of the Bell'). In 1880 he succeeded his compatriot Julius Benedict to take up the appointment of conductor, chorus master and pianoforte accompanist with the orchestra. As the *Liverpool Mail* reported at the time: 'Herr Max Bruch's duties at Liverpool involve a weekly rehearsal and twelve concerts per season. The salary is £400 a year, and the conductor guarantees to reside in Liverpool for at least seven months in every year.'

Bruch's appointment was by the unanimous decision of the Philharmonic Society's committee, but it was not welcomed by everybody. The writer of a letter in the *Liverpool Mail* in April 1880, signing himself 'A Citizen', was not happy with the 'selection of Max Bruch instead of an Englishman for the conductorship of the Philharmonic Society'. The same newspaper published a scathing article on the committee's decision:

> With a curiously cynical indifference to the dictates of propriety and the feeling of the public, the Philharmonic committee have appointed as their new conductor a stranger in the person of Mr Max Bruch. The decision may have caused little surprise to those who know the composition of the committee, and are aware how thoroughly it is dominated by the foreigners who find place amongst its members. The selection of a conductor appears to

have been left mainly, if not entirely, to a sub-committee, of which the guiding light was Mr H. E. Rensburg - a passionate and confirmed Teuto-maniac - and when this sub-committee presented recommendation in favour of Mr Max Bruch their present might seem to have been meekly accepted by the main body without a word by way either of question or protest. We cannot compliment the English members of the committee upon the spirit they have displayed; and if gentlemen of their lofty intellects will condescend to test the feeling of the public generally we venture to think that even they will be struck with the unanimity and the vigour with which our view is endorsed. The annual meeting of the society is approaching, and when that event takes place it is to be hoped that some subscriber may be found possessed of more courage than the faint-hearted Englishmen of the committee. It may be too late to reverse the decision which has been come to. Indeed, to do would be an ungracious act, and one that is not to be recommended; but an expression of opinion should go forth with force unmistakable enough to render the committee more regardful in the future of their clear and direct duty.

We do not wish to under-estimate the abilities of Mr Max Bruch, or any other foreign musician. Mr Bruch is a composer of talent and rank; but, in appointing him as their conductor, the Philharmonic committee have deliberately preferred to take a leap in the dark, when reason and justice alike demanded that they should know where they were stepping. What knowledge have they of Mr Bruch's capacities as a conductor, beyond, indeed, that which may have been obtained at second hand from prejudiced testimony? And granting, for the sake of argument, that Mr Bruch is an efficient conductor, is an almost total ignorance of the English tongue an obstacle which can be overcome so lightly? Before he assumes the conductor's chair, Mr Bruch if our information be right, should go to school to acquire the very rudiments of the language in which his choral forces are to sing. The clumsy gutturals of an Anglo-German *patois* afford a dubious medium in which to convey to Englishmen a true perception of the subtleties of their national music.

Regarded in whatever light, the selection of Mr Bruch is a mistake. We say it with the readiest acknowledgment of the gentleman's talent as a composer. But there is a place for all men, and in appointing Mr Max Bruch as the conductor of their concerts the committee of the Philharmonic Society have been guilty of a culpable indifference to this axiom, which should not escape the indignant notice either of the subscribers to the concerts or of the public at large.

Bruch's first few months in Liverpool were lonely; he missed his fiancée Clara Tuczek, to whom he had become engaged in August 1880 in Berlin. His mood was soon to change for the better. In December 1880, Bruch returned to Berlin for Christmas, and in January 1881 married his beloved Clara before travelling back with her to Liverpool. The *Liverpool Mail* approved: 'Miss Tuczek, who is an accomplished musician, is reported to possess a beautiful alto voice, and no doubt her residence in Liverpool will prove a desirable acquisition to local musical circles.'

Among the works Bruch introduced to Liverpool for the first time were Glinka's Symphony on Two Russian Themes, Mozart's Sinfonia Concertante, Berlioz's *Harold in Italy* and Cowen's Scandinavian Symphony. In 1881 he presented Handel's Messiah at St George's Hall,[8] conducting there for the first time and engaging a chorus of around 250 singers.

Naturally, there were performances of Bruch's own choral, instrumental and concerted works, most for the first time at Philharmonic Hall. He presented his oratorio *Odysseus* again (after its performance in 1877), with his wife singing the part of Penelope.

By all accounts Bruch was a perfectionist and autocrat, and he was soon to earn a reputation for his bad temper and boorish behaviour.

---

[8] 'One of the world's great edifices', St George's Hall was built for 'Arts, Laws and Counsel'. This fine example of Greco-Roman architecture was designed by Harvey Lonsdale Elmes and is dated 1854.

According to an article in the *Liverpool Mercury* in 1899: 'There were several matters which mitigated against the success of Max Bruch in Liverpool. He knew but little English at first, and his manner was not conciliatory at the best.'

His artistic temperament may often have been an impediment in his relationship with colleagues, but there is evidence that behind Bruch's forbidding exterior lay a generous nature. He is known to have performed many a kindly action, particularly in the service of a fellow musician. To borrow James Boswell's description of Dr Johnson: 'Though there was a roughness in his manner, there was no ill nature in his disposition.'

As comfortable and at ease in his domestic situation as he appeared to be, Bruch's professional life was becoming less agreeable. He was clearly unhappy in his post: as an artist of fine sensibilities, he was unable to cope well with the everyday duties required of him. In 1883, before the season was over, he tendered his resignation. The book *Two Centuries of Music in Liverpool* (Taylor, S. de B.) tells us that he left behind him a 'a choir whose morale was temporarily broken, a bewildered orchestra and a sharply divided committee of management'. In January 1883, the *Liverpool Echo* printed the following item:

We much regret to have to announce that the Liverpool Philharmonic Society is about to lose the highly-valued services of the distinguished composer who, as conductor, has shed lustre on its recent history as a musical institution. In the course of the last month, Mr Max Bruch received the offer of the position of conductor of the concerts in Breslau, the capital of Silesia, and the largest provincial town in Germany. After very careful consideration, Mr Bruch came to the decision to accept this honourable offer, and to give up his position in Liverpool. His intention having always been to return sooner or later to his native land, Mr Bruch felt that he could not refuse so favourable an opportunity, one which might not have been offered again for many years. On Wednesday the resignation was tendered to the

62

Philharmonic committee, and it is now a fait accompli. In addressing the committee of the Philharmonic Society, Mr Max Bruch wrote: 'I intend and hope to visit England frequently in the future, and I trust it may be my good fortune to keep up those friendly relations with the Liverpool Philharmonic Society which I value so very highly.' The regret created by the intelligence now communicated to the public will be deep and general, and Mr Max Bruch will be attended to his new sphere by the heartiest good wishes for his future prosperity and distinction.

Apart from the *Scottish Fantasy*, it is through another of his most memorable and enduring compositions that Max Bruch is linked to the city of Liverpool. Though conceived in Berlin, *Kol Nidrei: Adagio after Hebrew Themes for Violoncello and Orchestra* was completed during his tenure with the Liverpool Philharmonic and premièred in Liverpool. It was dedicated to the German cellist Robert Hausmann. 'Kol Nidrei' is a Hebrew prayer sung in synagogues on the eve of Yom Kippur, the Day of Atonement.[9] Bruch took this haunting melody and developed it with a contrasting theme from the moving song 'Oh weep for those that wept on Babel's stream' from George Gordon Byron's *Hebrew Melodies*. (Like Maurice Ravel, Bruch was a non-Jew who composed on Jewish themes.) *Kol Nidrei* was an immediate success and Bruch wrote an arrangement of the piece for violin and piano. Versions also appeared for solo piano, viola and piano and other instruments.[10]

---

[9] The prayer 'Kol Nidrei' (כָּל נִדְרֵי), Aramaic for 'All Vows', is actually a legal formula nullifying any vows, oaths or pledges made since the previous Yom Kippur, or that might be made in the following year.
[10] In 1938 the Jewish composer Arnold Schoenberg wrote a liturgical work *Kol Nidre,* a setting of the same prayer for mixed chorus, speaker, and orchestra.

FANTASIA (Op. 46)...*Max Bruch.*

For Violin (Orchestra and Harp), with free adaptation
of Scotch Melodies.

I. INTRODUCTION and ADAGIO.
II. SCHERZO (DANCE).
III. ANDANTE.
IV. ALLEGRO GUERRIERO.

(First performance in England.)

Herr JOACHIM.

Scottish Fantasy, 22 February 1881

SOLI VIOLONCELLO.

(*a*) " Kol Nidrei" (Hebrew Melody.) ...*Max Bruch.*
(With ORCHESTRA.)

(*b*) " Perpetuum mobile." ....*Fitzenhagen.*

(*c*) " Abendlied." ....*Schumann.*

Mr. HAUSMANN.

Kol Nidrei, 7 February 1882

Detail from Liverpool Philharmonic Society Concert Programmes

Other works completed by Bruch in his Liverpool period were *Three Hebrew Songs* for chorus and orchestra, *Four Choruses* for male voice choir, and the seven songs entitled *Lieder und Gesänge*, dedicated to his wife Clara.

When Bruch conducted the first UK performance of the *Scottish Fantasy* at a concert in Liverpool on 21 February 1881, the *Liverpool Mercury* advertised the work as 'The Fantasia on Scotch Airs'. The soloist on this occasion was Bruch's friend and collaborator Joseph Joachim and the harpist was William Streather. The composer was disappointed with Joachim's rendition, commenting that 'in the Scherzo, he lacked Sarasate's incomparable charm and grace, the *cantilena* in the first and third movements were too restless, the series of trills in the Finale were slow, and the top notes were completely missed.'

The programme included Schubert's Unfinished Symphony and music by Spohr, as well as two orchestral marches by Joachim, which he conducted himself. A review of the concert in the *Liverpool Daily Post* was favourable to the *Scottish Fantasy,* but its assessment of Joachim's playing was at odds with Bruch's own:

A prominent feature of the programme was a fantasia for violin, harp, and orchestra, by the conductor, produced for the first time in England last evening and enjoying the double advantage of the superintendence of the composer, and of the violin part being rendered by Herr Joachim. The fantasia was mainly built on Scotch melodies, but Herr Max Bruch is entitled to great praise for the skilful manner in which he has treated the melodies, and for the picturesque and clever orchestration with which he has surrounded them. The instrumentation and general treatment evince much musicianly feeling, and the only question one is disposed to ask, is, would not Herr Bruch have been better advised in expending his ability and imaginativeness upon original subject matter? Herr Joachim played the solo portion of the work with exquisite delicacy and tenderness and invested his part with great beauty and importance by the consummate charm of his playing.

While living in Liverpool with his wife, Bruch's residence was a large, three-storey, double-fronted Victorian house in Brompton Avenue, a street of similar properties in the residential district of Sefton Park. Although he may not have been entirely happy in the city, Bruch would have found himself in congenial surroundings in a convenient location, being close to Liverpool's largest public park and just a short trip by horse and carriage to Philharmonic Hall.[11]

In the words of the *Liverpool Mercury*: 'It is only a pity that, possessed of such inborn kindliness of nature, the German musician's career should have been so unsatisfactory, from a public point of view, in our city.' Nevertheless, Liverpool has been left with a legacy of fine music as a reminder of its association with a great artist.

Liverpool Philharmonic Hall in Bruch's day

---

[11] The original Philharmonic Hall was opened in 1849 and burnt down in 1933. A new concert hall, in Art Deco style, was built on the same site and this, with some alterations, is the building that stands today.

DESERT ISLAND DISCS

esert Island Discs started on BBC radio in January 1942 and is one of the world's longest continuously running radio programmes. It was devised by broadcaster and writer Roy Plomley, who presented the programme for 43 years. The celebrity guests - who have ranged from stage and film actors, sports stars and writers to musicians, politicians and royalty - are asked to choose the 8 records they would take to an imaginary desert island.

To date more than 3000 editions of the programme have been broadcast, and they have included a range of music as diverse as the people choosing it. While Bruch's G minor Violin Concerto has featured numerous times, only three 'castaways' have chosen the *Scottish Fantasy* among their selection of music. It is surprising that such a lovely work is not more widely known. (This fact is evident in the annual Classic FM Radio 'Hall of Fame' poll of listeners' favourite classical music. Though not a scientific survey, it provides an indication of popular taste. The G Minor Concerto has regularly featured in the top 3, whereas the *Scottish Fantasy* seldom reaches the top 100.)

The three guests who chose the *Scottish Fantasy* as one of their desert island discs were Isaac Stern, Molly Weir and Joan Baez.

Isaac Stern, Violinist (b. 1920, Kremenetz, Ukraine; d. 2001, New York, NY, USA)

Isaac Stern was a master violinist, educator and ambassador for his art. He moved to the United States at an early age and performed with the San Francisco Symphony Orchestra at the age of 11. He made over 100 recordings and had many contemporary works composed for him by, among others, Leonard Bernstein, Krzysztof Penderecki, George Rochberg and Peter Maxwell Davies.

Apart from his classical work, he also enjoyed playing lighter pieces and recorded a number of albums. He made many television appearances, and he provided the solo violin on the soundtrack of the films *Humoresque* (1946) and *Fiddler on the Roof* (1971). He appeared as himself in the film *Music of the Heart* (1999).

8 January 1972, speaking to Roy Plomley.
(Jascha Heifetz, New Symphony Orchestra of London, Sir Malcolm Sargent)

'As far as I am concerned, if they write the history of the violin there are three names that will have to be there forever: they're Paganini, Ysaÿe and Heifetz. And what is certainly one of the great performances on the violin is the *Scottish Fantasy* of Bruch as played by Jascha Heifetz.'

Molly Weir, British Actress (b. 1910, Glasgow; d. 2004, London)

A familiar Scottish voice on radio and television, Molly Weir found fame in 1950 when she was offered the part of Aggie the housekeeper in *Life With The Lyons,* a successful sitcom starring the Hollywood double act Ben Lyon and Bebe Daniels.

She made appearances in dozens of other series on television in the 1950s and 1960s and in several British films, including *Flesh and Blood* (1951) and *John and Julie* (1955).

8 October 1977, speaking to Roy Plomley.
(David Oistrakh, London Symphony Orchestra, Jascha Horenstein)

'I chose this record because at home when we're a wee bit homesick this is the one we put on. And I want the nice third movement which is described as evocative and nostalgic, and I can lose myself with misty dreams of the Highlands and Islands. David Oistrakh playing, I think, because I heard him at the Albert Hall and I thought his violin playing was quite magnificent.'

Joan Baez, Folksinger and Songwriter (b. 1941, New York)

The singer and musician Joan Baez became part of the US music scene after appearing at the 1959 Newport Folk Festival. She was popular with young audiences in the 1960s for her songs and as a protest figure, going on to make many hit albums.

As part of her campaigning, she gave free concerts supporting civil rights and UNESCO, and took part in anti-Vietnam war rallies. Joan Baez has recorded songs in several languages and performed publicly for more than six decades.

20 June 1993, speaking to Sue Lawley.
(Jascha Heifetz, New Symphony Orchestra of London, Sir Malcolm Sargent)

'It really is because of Heifetz. And because I heard this particular piece over and over again. But Heifetz to me is the ultimate violinist.'

David Oistrakh

Jascha Heifetz

Kyung-Wha Chung

Arthur Grumiaux

Itzhak Perlman

Tasmin Little

Scottish Fantasy on Vinyl, Cassette, CD and Video

RECORDINGS MADE OF SCOTTISH FANTASY

'A Scottish song, thus performed, is among the highest of entertainments to a musical genius. But is this genius to be acquired either in the performer or hearer? It cannot. Genius in music, as in poetry, is the gift of Heaven.'

Favourite Scots Songs
W. Tytler

The first commercial recording of the *Scottish Fantasy* was by Jascha Heifetz in 1939. He recorded it again in 1947 and 1954, and in 1971 recorded a video performance in Paris for his 70th birthday, acting as conductor as well as soloist. (There is also a recording on 78rpm sound discs of Heifetz playing the *Scottish Fantasy* on the The Bell Telephone Hour radio programme in 1947 with the Bell Telephone Orchestra.) On all occasions he performs a truncated version of the work, with passages cut from the second and final movements. Unfortunately, this is a practice that has continued in many subsequent recordings (and concert performances); and it is one which Bruch aficionados might properly consider a travesty. (In his recording with the London Symphony Orchestra, one of the finest, David Oistrakh plays the complete version.) To date, the only other violinists to have recorded the work more than once are David Oistrakh and Itzhak Perlman.

Not all elite violinists have committed an interpretation of the *Scottish Fantasy* to record. One wonders what nuances of tone and phrasing such masters as Mischa Elman, Leonid Kogan, Nathan

Milstein or Ida Haendel would have brought to the work.

As its subtitle suggests, the work contains a prominent part for the harp, which provides important accompaniment throughout the four movements. In some recordings the soloist is focused so closely that the playing of the harp is all but drowned out. In addition, recording notes seldom mention the name of the harpist. Once again, David Oistrakh's recording is an exception. In it we hear the playing of the renowned Welsh harpist Osian Ellis, whose contribution is suitably acknowledged alongside soloist, orchestra and conductor.

Every known commercial recording of the *Scottish Fantasy* made to date is listed below. (Note that some recordings may also have been issued on other labels. The year shown is the year of recording or first release.)

SALVATORE ACCARDO, Leipzig Gewandhaus Orchestra, Kurt Masur (Decca, 1977)

JOSHUA BELL, Academy of St Martin in the Fields, dir. Joshua Bell (Sony, 2018)

'There's persuasive urgency as well as sweetness, for example, in his playing of the tune "Through the wood, laddie" in the first movement. And while his Scherzo feels stodgy compared with some rival accounts, I find the coy, almost sexy way Bell shapes the grazioso passage utterly irresistible.' (*Gramophone Magazine*)

NICOLA BENEDETTI, BBC Scottish Symphony Orchestra, cond. Rory Macdonald (Decca, 2014)

'Her assured technique sees her through all the formidable obstacles en route...The BBC Scottish SO conducted by Rory MacDonald share Benedetti's rapport with this music, playing from the heart.' (*Gramophone Magazine*)

GUY BRAUNSTEIN, Bamberger Symphoniker, cond. Ion Marin (Tudor, 2013)

[ALFREDO] CAMPOLI, London Philharmonic Orchestra, cond. Sir Adrian Boult (Decca, 1958)

'The work has no need of heroic postures; it is concerned with lyrical themes and delicate ornaments, and nobody can bring these off more perfectly than Campoli, whose tone is always pure and sweet.' (*The Stereo Record Guide*)

KYUNG-WHA CHUNG, Royal Philharmonic Orchestra, cond. Rudolph Kempe (Decca, 1972)

'[Kyung-Wha Chung] transcends the episodic nature of the writing to give the music a genuine depth and concentration, above all in the lovely slow movement. Kempe and the Royal Philharmonic, not always perfectly polished, give sympathetic accompaniment.' (*Penguin Cassette Guide*)

JAMES EHNES, Montreal Symphony Orchestra, Mario Bernardi (CBC, 2002)

MAXIM FEDOTOV, Russian Philharmonic Orchestra, cond. Dmitry Yablonsky (Naxos, 2003)

'Maxim Fedotov may be a little short on mystery and tenderness, but his bravura playing, helped by full-blooded accompaniment from Dmitry Yablonsky, makes the results consistently compelling.' (*The Gramophone Classical Music Guide*)

NING FENG, Deutsches Symphonie-Orchester Berlin, cond. (Channel Classics, 2014)

ARTHUR GRUMIAUX, New Philharmonia Orchestra, cond. Heinz Wallberg (Philips, 1974)

MAURICE HASSON, Scottish National Orchestra, Alexander Gibson (Classics For Pleasure, 2012)

JASCHA HEIFETZ, RCA Victor Symphony Orchestra, cond. William Steinberg, Laura Newell, harp (RCA, 1939)

JASCHA HEIFETZ, London Philharmonic Orchestra, Sir John Barbirolli (Naxos, 1947)

'Bruch's *Scottish Fantasy* was always a favourite work with Heifetz, and although his pioneering 1947 version cannot quite match his stereo remake with Sargent and the LSO in thoughtful intensity, the passion and brilliance of the playing are most compelling, with the songful *Adagio* section even more moving in its simpler, more flowing manner, hushed and dedicated.' (*The Penguin Guide to Recorded Classical Music*)

JASCHA HEIFETZ, New Symphony Orchestra of London, cond. Sir Malcolm Sargent (RCA, 1954)

JASCHA HEIFETZ, Orchestre National de France, dir. Jascha Heifetz (BMG Classics, 1971)

ULF HOELSCHER, Bamberger Symphoniker, cond. Bruno Weil (Warner Classics, 2011)

SABRINA-VIVIAN HÖPCKER, Nordwestdeutsche Philharmonie, cond. Edwin Outwater (True Sounds, 2009)

YUZUKO HORIGOME, Royal Philharmonic Orchestra, cond. Yuri Simonov (Classics, 1995)

JACK LIEBECK, BBC Scottish Symphony Orchestra, cond. Martyn Brabbins (Hyperion, 2014)

CHO-LIANG LIN, Chicago Symphony Orchestra, Leonard Slatkin (Sony, 1987)

'Lin is technically pretty well flawless but what impresses most is the way he takes the music at face value: by not playing to the gallery he manages to make the work's sentimentality seem touching rather than sugary.' (*Gramophone Magazine*)

TASMIN LITTLE, Royal Scottish National Orchestra, Vernon Handley (Classics for Pleasure, 1997)

'Tasmin Little takes a ripe, robust and passionate view of the work, projecting it strongly, as she would in the concert hall. In this she is greatly helped by the fine, polished playing of the Scottish orchestra under Vernon Handley, a most sympathetic partner.' (*The Penguin Guide to Compact Discs & DVDs*)

VANESSA-MAE, London Symphony Orchestra, cond. Viktor Fedotov (EMI, 1996)

ANNE AKIKO MEYERS, Royal Philharmonic Orchestra, cond. Jesús López Cobos (RCA, 1992)

MIDORI, Israel Philharmonic Orchestra, cond. Zubin Mehta (Sony, 1993)

DAVID OISTRAKH, State Symphony Orchestra of USSR, Gennady Rozhdestvensky (Praga Digitals, 1960)

DAVID OISTRAKH, London Symphony Orchestra, cond. Jascha Horenstein, Osian Ellis, harp (Decca, 1963)

'The Oistrakh/Horenstein performance completely displaces its competitors. The expansive dignity of the opening of the brass sets shows immediately how fine the orchestral contribution is going to be and Oistrakh's playing throughout is ravishing, raising the stature of the work immeasurably.' (*The Stereo Record Guide*)

ITZHAK PERLMAN, New Philharmonia Orchestra, cond. Jesús López Cobos (EMI, 1976)

'Perlman's account of the delightful Scottish Fantasia is wholly delectable, showing the same degree of stylish lyricism and eloquence of phrasing.' (*Penguin Cassette Guide*)

ITZHAK PERLMAN, Israel Philharmonic Orchestra, cond. Zubin Mehta (EMI, 1988)

RACHEL BARTON PINE, Scottish Chamber Orchestra, cond. Alexander Platt (Cedille Records, 2005)

ELIZABETH PITCAIRN, Sofia Philharmonic Orchestra, cond. Maxim Eshkenazy (CD Baby, 2007)

MICHAEL RABIN, Philharmonia Orchestra, cond. Adrian Boult (Columbia, 1960)

'Transcendental.' (*Great Violinists in Performance*)

AARON ROSAND, NDR Radio-Philharmonie Hannover, cond. Christoph Wyneken (Biddulph, 2020)

BENJAMIN SCHMID, Orchester Musikkollegium Winterthur, cond. Jac van Steen (OEHMS, 2003)

AKIKO SUWANAI, Academy of St Martin in the Fields, cond. Sir Neville Marriner (Philips, 1996)

JANUSZ WAWROWSKI, Stuttgarter Philharmoniker, cond.
Daniel Raiskin (Warner Classics, 2017)
ANTJE WEITHAAS (violin) NDR Radiophilharmonie, cond.
Hermann Bäumer (CPO, 2013)

There is also a recording (not commercially available) of a sensitive reading by Lydia Mordkovitch, ably supported by the BBC Scottish Symphony Orchestra, conducted by Jerzy Maksymiuk.

A variety of video and audio recordings of the work are available on the YouTube website.

REFERENCES

A Selection of the most Favourite Scots Songs, W. Tytler (William Napier, 1790)

British Newspaper Archive

Dessert Island Lists, Roy Plomley with Derek Drescher (Hutchinson, 1984)

Early Scottish Melodies, John Glen (J. & R. Glen, 1900)

Great Violinist in Performance, Henry Roth (Panjandrum Books, 1987)

Europeana: Hamburg State Library

Liverpool Record Office: Liverpool Philharmonic Society Archive

Master Violinist in Performance, Henry Roth (Paganiniana Publications, Inc., 1982)

Max Bruch: His Life and Works, Christopher Fifield (The Boydell Press, 1988)

Pablo Sarasate, El Violín de Europa, María Nagore Ferrer (2009)

Pablo Sarasate: Un Violinista Inmortal, Pablo Ransanz (2008)

Poems and Songs by Robert Burns (Bell and Daldy, 1858)

Scottish Fantasy in Full Score (Dover Publications, Inc., 2011)

The Book of Scottish Songs, Alex Whitelaw (Blackie & Son, 1843)

The New Grove Dictionary of Music and Musicians, Stanley Sadie (Ed.) (Macmillan Publishers Ltd., 2001)

The Penguin Cassette Guide, Edward Greenfield, Robert Layton and Ivan March (Penguin Books, 1979)

The Penguin Guide to Compact Discs & DVDs, Edward Greenfield, Robert Layton and Ivan March (Penguin Books, 2003)

The Poems & Songs of Robert Burns, with a New Sketch of his Life (Wilson, McCormick and Carnie, 1819)

The Scotish [sic] *Musical Museum 1787,* James Johnson (William Blackwood and Sons, 1839)

The Songs of Scotland (Maurice Ogle and Company, 1871)

The Stereo Record Guide, Edward Greenfield, Robert Layton and Ivan March (The Long Playing Record Library Ltd., 1972)

Two Centuries of Music in Liverpool, Stainton de Boufflers Taylor (Rockliff Brothers Ltd., 1976)

Violin Mastery, Frederick H. Martens (Ed.) (Dover Publications, Inc., 2006)

INDEX OF NAMES

INDEX OF SCOTTISH SONGS

INDEX OF SCOTTISH WORKS